T0196224

What Happens to Me after He's Gone

A Financial Survival Guide for Pastor's Wives and Women Everywhere

Vera L. Lewis

authorHOUSE®

AuthorHouse™
1663 Liberty Drive
Bloomington, IN 47403
www.authorhouse.com
Phone: 1-800-839-8640

First published by AuthorHouse   11/14/2011

ISBN: 978-1-4678-7686-5 (sc)
ISBN: 978-1-4678-7685-8 (ebk)

Library of Congress Control Number: 2011960923

Printed in the United States of America

Any people depicted in stock imagery provided by Thinkstock are models, and such images are being used for illustrative purposes only. Certain stock imagery © Thinkstock.

This book is printed on acid-free paper.

Contents

Dedication

This book is dedicated to my husband, the late Pastor James David Lewis. He loved what he was called to do: to preach the Gospel of Jesus Christ without compromise. He was the epitome of a man of God, who always walked in integrity and lived what he preached. He was a great pastor, husband, father, grandfather, son, brother, uncle, and friend to all who knew him.

We love you and miss you. Your legacy lives on in our hearts and through the lives you touched. You left us much too soon!

I also dedicate this book to those widows who shared their stories with me so that other women might benefit from their ill fortunes and never have to suffer the same catastrophes they endured after the deaths of their husbands. May their testimonies be a source of light and awareness to the world regarding the neglectfulness and unconscionable lack of care and concern for these women of valor, faithfulness, undeniable worth, and wisdom. Know that "the Lord has heard the voice of your weeping" (Ps. 6:8b NKJV), and he understands the language of your tears. May the mercies of God intercede for you and sustain you as you now prepare for this unfamiliar journey of life.

Acknowledgments

With special thanks to the Vera Lewis Ministries team for your continuous love, prayers, and support for the time dedicated to the research, typing, and editing. Your tireless and diligent hard work made this project possible.

To my mother, Willie B. Simon, for always covering me in prayer.

To my children, grandchildren, and entire family for just being there.

To Mother Freddie Carter, the late supervisor of Texas Northeast 1, who always believed in me and encouraged me to finish this endeavor.

Introduction

Proverbs 15:25 says, "The Lord will destroy the house of the proud but he will establish the border of the widow" (KJV).

When evil men try to take the property of widows, God will intervene (MacArthur 1997, 898). I feel a clarion call to take a humble but strong stand as His intervention for this generation and generations to come, stopping the unnecessary oppression, heartache, and financial hardship that have been tolerated for much too long.

Many widows, especially pastors' wives, are the silent victims that no one wants to listen to or deal with. We are expected to sit quietly by, say nothing, and certainly not do anything. Our worlds as we know them are turned upside down.

I encourage women everywhere to take action as the catalyst for this era and to be ready for the unpredictable change in their tomorrows. Read these chapters and see them as your convoy for a more secure, settled, and happy future.

Prayer

Lord, I present this book to you and pray that every scripted word will send an awakening evangelistic message to the spirit and minds of both men and women throughout the world to accept the obligation of preparing to live as well as preparing to die. Help us, heavenly Father, as we go about doing kingdom work and building ministries, help us to do it with excellence, wisdom, and integrity and not forget to make provisions for those we love after we are gone. Lord, I pray that not another widow will have to cry herself to sleep at night because of the prominence of *not enough*. Let the amen of God confirm these words and establish your future. Amen.

There Is a Word

Exodus 22:22–23 (KJV)

> "Ye shall not afflict any widow or fatherless child. If thou afflict them in any wise, and they cry at all unto me, I will surely hear their cry."

Chapter 1
Ready or Not He's Gone

Whether you are now alone because of the death of a spouse or the experience of divorce, the fact remains that you must deal with what is to come. For many, the shadows of uncertainty are almost overwhelming; pastors' wives and women in general are left with too little too soon, and then the ordeal of drastic changeover begins. Even in the twenty-first century, no one knows quite what to do with us after our husbands pass away.

In most denominations, a pastor's wife is usually given the unofficial designation as first lady. Having worn the title of first lady and then Evangelist Vera Lewis, after my husband's death, it was decided that I would be called Cofounder Lewis. This seemed fitting, since my husband and I founded Bethlehem Church of God in Christ thirty-five years ago. I co-labored with my husband, giving years of service, sacrifice, and struggle. Now that my title was settled, I wondered where I would go from there. Only time would tell. I felt lost and out of place in an environment where I had once felt at ease and at home. As I walked this new walk of sublime faithfulness with an all-knowing God, my life was in His hands.

No longer, no longer, no longer—I repeat again—no longer can we stand idly by and not strategically place a plan into operation for such a time as this. A period of heartbreak, distress, bewilderment, confusion, and transition sets in all at once. It is so traumatic that it sends you into the deepest depths of depression and immobilizes you both mentally and physically. Just to get out of bed becomes the most arduous task to conquer. You ask yourself, "What do I do now?" Is there some kind of guide on how to live when you can't even feel your heart beat? How do you go on alone without that soul partner you depended on spiritually, emotionally, and financially?

Believe me when I say that grieving is a lot easier if you are not homeless, hungry, or helpless! I have not experienced any of these particular misfortunes, but there are too many women who have. I know of one former first lady who at age seventy recently retired from a school cafeteria where she had worked for twelve years just to make ends meet after her husband passed. She was only fifty-seven years old when her husband died, and prior to his death she had been a stay-at-home mom for fifteen years. She had worked diligently with her husband to build their ministry. Her life went on a downward spiral upon his death; she was angry and bitter, with no means to sustain herself or provide for her children and no support from the church.

It is not the will of God for those women who have co-labored with their husbands faithfully for years to be quietly discharged at their husbands' gravesites without even a notable mention. Many of them become so disillusioned and distraught afterward that they never find their places in life again. Their lives as pastor's wives is all some of them had for years, and then they are unofficially silenced and cast aside within their own houses. Their spirits are broken as they drift out of sight and out of the minds of those to whom they had given so much. But in my case, I was determined to make a destiny decision to survive against all odds. Little can be done for what has happened to those pastors' wives in the past, but something can and must be done about the lives of these women today, and it starts with us.

The title *poor and pitiful widow* need never be attached to your identity. *Abused, neglected,* and *ousted* must never be your garments of mourning or your cloaks of shame. Our husbands have gone on to be with the Lord, but we're still here. And there's much work to be done. You are valuable to the kingdom of God.

Through all the perplexities, through all the temptations, through all the insurmountable problems, and by the grace of God, you're going to make it. It does not matter what has happened or how unnerving and disheartening the situation. I am a witness that God will give you the ability to stand and persevere when everything in your life goes absolutely crazy and your world turns upside down. The tides of boisterous, troubled waters almost drown us, and the velocity of tempestuous winds knocks us to our knees; we are almost shattered by the turbulence of circumstance that shakes our very foundations, taking our breaths away. The person who was your soul tie, the person in whom you had found happiness and security is now gone, never to return, but you must go on. Weep for that which is lost if you must, but do not allow the flood of tears to blind you so that you cannot see that you still have a future and a purpose.

Many of you are like me: married almost all of your adult lives. Your identity is so connected with that union that, without that significant other, the sense of displacement, bewilderment, and loneliness you feel at life's unpredictable whirlwind of change is mind-boggling. This is where you have to give the Lord hallelujah anyhow praise. You might not feel like it, and you might not understand the why of what's happening, but praise Him anyhow. I thank God that I'm still here and that I did not lose my mind. Send the devil an announcement: it's not over, and you will be back stronger than ever. Only the living God can revive you again, increase your greatness, and comfort you on every side (Ps. 71:20–21).

Your praise will bring you out of the depths of despair and the dungeon of depression. You are not alone in how you're feeling. What you're feeling is normal for what you're going through in this season of re-establishment. Don't focus so much on what has happened or what you're going through, but rather focus on the one Savior who is able to bring you out. When He brings you out, you won't even look like you were in bondage. He will bring out everything connected to you. Don't lose your faith now; don't have a nervous breakdown; and don't throw in the towel. You might feel like a female Job, like you have lost it all, but be encouraged, for the Lord knows when you can't stand to lose another thing. This is when you find out what you are made of. You can get in bed, cover your head, and allow the changeability of circumstances to immobilize you with fear and self-pity, or you can *decide* to live out the rest of your days with purpose and fulfillment and not to leave out happiness, peace, joy, goodness, gentleness, kindness, temperance and all that the spirit produces (Gal. 5:22).

Prayer

Lord, I pray that the women reading this book will find a new revelation dealing with their business matters as never before. Open their eyes and let them see what must be done and prepare them with your guiding hand for the changes that are coming in their lives. Give unto these women the courage, perseverance and wisdom to continue on even as they walk alone. Lord consulate these souls one and all. Let your hand heal the wounds. Amen.

There Is a Word

Psalm 90:15 (LB)

> "Give us gladness in proportion to our former misery! Replace the evil years with good."

Chapter 2
Be Prepared for the Unexpected

"You do not know what will happen tomorrow" (James 4:14 NKJV). It is important that you make preparations for the unexpected and do it now. Not tomorrow but *now!* Tomorrow could be too late. Ask your husband these life-saving questions regarding your future welfare:

1. What happens to me after you are gone?
2. How will I live?
3. Where will I live?
4. Will I be able to maintain my present lifestyle?

If he cannot answer you with a designated plan of protection for financial support at his death, you are in so much *T-R-O-U-B-L-E!* If your husband does not say that you can expect guaranteed income for a specified period of time and that your home will be paid off and will remain yours, there is more planning to be done, starting today. You may have seen struggle before, but as this generation would say, "You ain't seen nothing yet!"

Ben Stein wrote in Newsmax.com article titled "For the Sake of Your Loved Ones, Get Life Insurance": "If husbands could take a moment to foresee what their potential widows' lives would be like without their regular paycheck or pension check, their very next call would be to their insurance agent" (2010). No one wants to think about the one appointment with death we all must keep. If you plan for this untimely visitation and prepare for this season of life, you can avoid the unwelcomed companions of anguish and frustration. The severity and unpredictability of life should encourage us all to be prepared both spiritually and financially at all times for whatever the tides of life may bring.

You are living well now because you and your husband have both labored and given birth to a ministry that has sustained you, and that's a good thing. But listen, ladies. Change can come overnight; one phone call can change your life forever. A trip to the doctor can transform your life forever, causing you to come face-to-face with the reality of immortality.

On December 7, 2007, that was my experience. My husband was diagnosed with multiple myeloma, a form of bone cancer and renal failure. In spite of the diagnosis, I always thought he would live. I would go to church and listen to him preach even when the cancer got to his legs and arms. He was then in a wheelchair, and the ministers of the church would hold his Bible and turn the pages for him as he told of the goodness of God. The congregation was still and quiet, for they did not want to miss a word spoken by this giant of a man and shepherd of souls. I walked in and looked around and said, "Lord, I know you are not going to take him now, not after all the labor, hard work, and sacrifice we put into this church. And now we finally got it just where we want it." The church was full, parking lot full, choir stand full, and every department functioning. "Not now God!" I insisted he was going to live, but I could see his suffering was becoming too much for him to bear. Sometimes we forget that man is like a breath; his days are like a passing shadow (Ps. 144:4 NKJV).

There will come a time when death will not bargain with you, compromise, or hear your cries for more time. For the time that was shall be no more. In spite of your accomplishments, scholastic achievements, talents, titles, preaching/teaching abilities, and even in spite of your righteousness, anointing, and the prayers of the saints, one must submit to the will of our God.

On December 7, 2008—exactly one year later—as I was sitting by my husband's side, God called him home with his family, friends, and church members singing hymns as he transferred from Earth to glory and into the arms of the waiting Savior. None of us know the day or the time He will choose to bring us home. That's God's business; that's not what this book is about. This book is to get your attention and move you into awareness and the position to prepare yourself for the unexpected. Be that twenty-first-century proverbial woman. Proverbs 31:25–27 says, she is a woman of strength and dignity and has no fear of old age. She watches carefully all that goes on throughout her household. She is a woman of wisdom and knowledge, knowing the business of her home, prepared for whatever happens.

The outdated notions of just letting others, even your spouse, handle everything and not knowing the business of your home or church will land you on Poverty Boulevard. You have gone through too much and co-labored with your husband for too long—struggling, sacrificing, praying, bringing many souls to Christ, organizing departments, frying too many chickens, selling too many dinners, putting on too many programs, and working up ministries and organizations—to live on that street. You deserve better in your latter days than in your former days. Blessed Lane belongs to you, my sister. You are not forgotten, and God remembers even though many whom you have helped, prayed for, and counseled with will fail to recollect or acknowledge you ever again. You have to know who you are and what you have contributed, and you must be prepared for the unexpected.

Prayer

Dear Lord, bless those who read these words with the insight and revelation that only you can give to prepare for the unexpectations of life. May they always drink from the wells that they have dug and never have to thirst or hunger as long as they live. Let the amen of God say so. Amen.

There Is a Word

1 Timothy 5:3 (KJV)

"Honour widows that are widows indeed."

Chapter 3
How Will You Live?

Will you be able to maintain your present lifestyle? If your husband should die now, what is your source of income? Will you have to do a 360° turn back into yesteryear, when *struggle* was your name and *never enough* was your calling card? All you had was mustard seed faith and a *yes Lord*. I don't know about you, but after the death of my husband, it was not my desire to even glance back into some of the hardships and struggles from which the Lord had brought us. Our home at that time was a one-bedroom apartment, we had three small children, and we could barely afford that. Our car was an old Volkswagen, which we scraped up two hundred dollars to buy, and that was our only means of transportation.

Our first church location was a one-room storefront with no air conditioning in the summer and no heat in the winter, but with the help of God we made it. We founded, built, and organized our ministry from the ground up. My husband was a young man with vision and a call from God to preach the gospel of Jesus Christ. Our first members were our children and immediate family members. After renting a storefront for several months, we moved into a better building where souls were saved. To our dismay, we found out that there was a lean on the property.

We then moved the service into our new home, where the bedrooms served as classrooms, and the garage was set up as the sanctuary. Even then the Lord continued to pour out His spirit. A young woman received the Holy Spirit in the garage. So many people came until our small home and the space to park was no longer sufficient. My husband located another building for worship. We then organized various departments, met the needs of the people, and served the community. We moved seven times before purchasing the property and then building at the location where our church stands today. The Lord had been good to us, and for that we were glad. The Lord blessed the work given to our hands, for He did promise to honor those who live to honor and serve Him.

Now we found ourselves flourishing and successful in that given call of predestined purpose. We were no longer struggling; neither were we wealthy, but surely we were most comfortable. Then death stepped into our midst and snatched my dear husband away—my love, my protector, my provider. In an instant, my life was turned upside down.

I used to sit up at night and wonder, *What shall I do? How do I live, not just emotionally but financially? Are there any provisions to protect me from creditors and predators that come to seek, take, and devour? What about the ministry that I gave my life to help establish? Will there be any continued support for me as "the wife" since he is gone? If so, how much is it, and is it enough to sustain my present lifestyle? How long will I receive compensation, if any? One month, six months, or a year?*

I, like many of you, had so many questions and so few answers. If you do not have the answers to these questions, I implore you to take action now so that you will always enjoy the sweet smell of security. You've earned it! Never ever leave your future preservation entirely in another individual's hands! Take care of your business now, and later your business will take care of you.

There are widows who did not receive anything after their husbands died. A story comes to mind of one pastor who was killed instantly in a tragic accident. The church he and his wife founded over thirty years ago, along with their church's newly appointed leader, decided not to provide any compensation to his widow. Her health insurance was canceled without her knowledge, leaving her with no means of getting the quality of care she was accustomed to. There was no one to fend for her and to make sure she was treated fairly. No covering is allotted to former first ladies, and you need to know this at the onset of your ministries. This might seem a little harsh to you, but this is reality.

Too many women, pastors' wives especially, are left with absolutely nothing but hard times and broken spirits. Psalm 69:20 states, "Reproach hath broken my heart; I am full of heaviness and I looked for some to take pity, but there was none, and for comforters, but I found none" (KJV). You must press into God as never before. Your sanity and your outcome will depend on it. I thought I knew God before my husband's death, but after it, I got to know Him at a level that I had never before encountered. I soon realized I trusted God, but my dependency upon my husband had always been my reserve.

Now I felt like a female Job. I had lost my father just six weeks before my husband's death. Everything as I had known it was no longer there. The loneliness was like a great hand that gripped my heart and wouldn't let go. At church, I stared blankly at his chair in the pulpit and envisioned him sitting there as he had for the previous thirty-two years. I looked for him to come in from the corridors as he always had and walk down the side aisle with the other elders. I longed to hear his strong voice sing his favorite song, "I'm Going to Trust in the Lord." But there was no song; he would never sing again. It was funny how his spirit seemed to be in the midst of service, but he wasn't there. I thought, *Lord, will I ever get past the pain I am feeling now?* Even in the midst of mass crowds, there was no release from the emptiness of my soul. I was like a sparrow alone on the housetop (Ps. 102:7 NKJV). David said he felt abandoned by man and God. No one understands the depth of your grief and, yes, disappointments.

The Lord understands the language of our tears, and no matter how fierce the battle, how heavy the load, He knows how much we can bear. You're not going to lose your mind, your joy, or your hope. I encourage you to get up, praise God, and live. It is a good time to draw near to God (Ps. 73:28). Let God have control of your new life. Calm down, and trust Him to see you through this most difficult period of readjustment. Commit yourself to keep moving during this time in your life.

We still have not solved this dilemma, but at least we are addressing this situation of placement and appropriate care of the widows of these great men of God. Take care of your business, and your business will later take care of you. When asked how you will manage, how you will live if something happens to your spouse, your reply will be, "I have a defined plan of security, and I will live *very well.*" Enjoy your now and your later!

Prayer

Dear Lord, in every aspect of our lives we seek your direction and your wisdom. Only you know what lies ahead for all of us. Teach us to number our days that we may gain a heart of wisdom. Lead and guide us in every decision we make. Then all will be well in our present and our futures.

I pray that leaders everywhere prepare for their families' welfare as they undertake the work of the cross. We bless your holy name. Amen.

There Is a Word

Isaiah 1:17(NKJV)

> "Learn to do good; Seek justice, Rebuke the oppressor: Defend the fatherless, plead for the widow."

Chapter 4
Where Will You Live?

Now that the funeral services are over, the transition of the church is settled, the mourning of others has ceased—though yours continues—and the calls are fewer and fewer, it is now time for a reality check. What about the house, the home where you raised your family or the dream home you and your husband bought and thought you would enjoy together for years to come? Is it really yours? Do you own it, or does the church own it?

I recently encountered a pastor's wife who once lived in the parsonage of the church. Almost immediately after the death of her husband, she was asked to move out. She was left searching for a place to live, with very little income. I have been blessed to remain in the home that my husband and I purchased fourteen years ago, but there are so many others who have not been as fortunate. Every woman should ask themselves, after the loss of your spouse, can you still afford the luxury of that beloved and familiar residence? Will there be enough income to meet this one most significant need?

Perhaps out of all the dreadful things that could happen to any woman is the loss of her home—her haven, her place of refuge. Every woman and man should get acquainted with these three words: *mortgage protection insurance*. Seal the acronym MPI inside your head and your heart. This means that at your spouse's death, your house is paid for and this load will not be yours to bear. Contact your mortgage company and ask about mortgage protection insurance. If you do not have it and you cannot get it, check to see if there is enough life insurance to cover your mortgage. At this point you can almost handle anything else that comes your way, as long as you have the assurance and peace of mind that your home is yours to keep, sell, or rent. It is yours without debate. Your home should be your castle, not your hassle.

Now, if the church has purchased your home, be ready for another reality check. When many pastors die, the churches have the authority to evict the pastors' wives after the pastors' deaths. Even the car that you're driving could not really be yours any longer if it was purchased by the church. They can repossess the keys from you at any given time, leaving you without any transportation, even though they bought the vehicle for you and the pastor.

Sometimes what seems easier can present a hardship to you as the pastor's wife if he dies before you do. It is a hard fact of life, but it is true. Some congregations will allow the former pastor's wife to keep the house and the car, but there are unfortunately too many that do not. Too many show no compassion or regard for the former pastor's family and leave them virtually destitute and distraught, with no place to live.

I am personally acquainted with several families who were forced to move out of their dream homes. One pastor's wife whose husband lost his battle with cancer was forced from her home with her two teenage children. She had no idea the home she lived in and the car she drove were owned by the church. After the death of her husband, she was asked to leave her home and return the car. She and her two teenage children moved into an apartment and had no transportation.

There is coverage for your car as well as your home that will allow them to be paid off at your spouse's death. Ladies, always know who really has the keys to your home and your car! Legally, lock the doors to your house and start the engine of your own car. God blessed you with these things, so keep and enjoy them. Don't let the enemy steal them from you!

Set your house in order now before it's too late. Know what you have and do not have. Also know what you're entitled to without any doubt. Avoid these words if at all possible: "I thought I had" or "I wish I had." These words could precede the anguish of not having enough to live on after he is gone. Be blessed, my sister, and enjoy the fruits of your labor even after he is no longer there. The emotional upheaval is enough without the stress of trying to survive financially.

Prayer

From this day on, I pray that not another one of my sisters will be heartbroken over this most unjustified and unmerited circumstance within their lives. My heavenly Father, show us what we need to do to set our affairs in order so that we may always enjoy the fruits of our labor. As they now walk alone, may it be without fear and poverty and oppression. May the mercy and the favor of God be with you. Amen.

There Is a Word

Acts 6:1(KJV)

> "And in those days, when the number of the disciples was multiplied, there arose a murmuring of the Grecians against the Hebrews, because their widows were neglected in the daily ministration."

Chapter 5
Invest Wisely

Might I encourage you to invest wisely? Putting your life savings into "you all's" ministry just may not be the wisest thing to do. You may be wondering, *why did she say "you all"?* I say that because it usually takes both spouses to sustain a ministry until it can thrive on its own. Both people are making huge sacrifices for the sake of building God's kingdom. Before you decide to invest your life savings, there are two things you should think about:

1) What if your husband dies prematurely by some unforeseen tragedy or accident? Should your husband die today and your savings has been depleted because you gave it all unselfishly to the church, are there means of support allocated just for you? Will you now depend on the new leader, deacons, and trustees of the church to remember the

generosity of your husband and the sacrifices you made? Unfortunately, this is very dangerous; you will be left with little or maybe no compensation without a financial plan in place.

2) What legal rights do you have to the financial investment you have made? Making a financial investment into your ministry is very noble and kind. However, first know that this is what God is leading you to do. Speak with your financial advisor for some practical insight before doing so. And of course, contact your attorney to discuss drafting a contractual document between you and your ministry. If you decided to take money from your retirement savings, you would want to know how and when the ministry will repay the loan. Although you don't need this money today, you may actually need it tomorrow. Perhaps this money should be returned to you with interest upon your husband's death or when your husband retires. You must consider that if this money would have been in a retirement savings account, it most likely would have gained some kind of interest.

I am sure you desire the prosperous life Jesus promised those who have labored in his vineyard. Statistics show that women live seven years longer than men, and over three quarters of all women are widowed at an average

age of fifty-six. Women comprise a horrifying 87 percent of the impoverished elderly (Bukow 2011). Also, women routinely don't save enough to survive on when they become widows—which 50 percent of us will be by the age of sixty. Of the elderly living in poverty, three out of four are women and 80 percent of these women were not poor when their husbands were alive (Kiyosaki 2011)!

"The wise woman builds her house" (Prov.14:1a KJV). Here are some tips for the wise women:

1) Be involved in the family finances. Know and understand what's going on with your investments, life insurance, and household expenses. Spend a few moments each week discussing finances with your spouse. If this is all new to you, start with making a list of all of your assets with account numbers as they exist today. List the details of the financial institution, log-in IDs and passwords, and the name(s) on the account; and most importantly, check if nominations are in place for each of them.

2) Keep organized records. Legal and important documents should be kept in a fire-proof safe at home or at a bank safety deposit box. Just make sure you can easily access them when needed.

3) Get professional financial advice. Don't wait until you need it. Speaking with a financial professional before life events happen will better prepare you

for the unexpected. If you do not have an advisor, interview at least three people. Remember, this should be a person you can trust and with whom you can build a relationship. You are probably saying now, "What questions do I ask?" Here are a few general questions; however, I strongly suggest that you do your own research to determine the questions that most interest you:

a) How long have you been a financial advisor?

b) Are you licensed to sell securities in the state you live?

c) What does your ideal client look like? (You want to know if they enjoy working with people like you.)

d) How do you make your money? (You want to know if this person is a fee-based advisor or commission only. Sometimes advisors will work both ways. This is not a secret. They should be willing to share this information with you.)

4) Your financial advisor can help you take a snapshot of where you are now in your financial life and help you determine your next steps. You will share your goals, your debt, your investment experience, and

what you want. As life changes, it is important that you share these life events with your advisor, as they can sometimes have an impact on your plan.

5) Hold on to your 401K. You will be glad you did it!

6) Spend money wisely. Have a plan. Just because you have money left at the end of the month doesn't mean you should go buy those new shoes and hats. Enjoy your shopping, but shop smart. A rainy day is coming.

Women of wisdom and valor arise and take your places now. Be the women that will stop this chain of pain and loss within our sisterhood of former first ladies and women everywhere. Be blessed my sister, always and forever. May the dividends of your investments bring outrageous benefits.

Prayer

Lord, I thank you for the insight to conduct business in an orderly and professional way so that our lives may be richer and fuller in spite of what comes. You are a God of wisdom, abundance, and direction. "Now though I may walk in the valley of the shadow of death, I will fear no evil: for thou art with me" (Ps. 23:4 KJV). Your truth consulates us today and always, and I will rejoice in the Lord. For the Lord God is our strength

Now, Lord, as we take a look at our work and our investments, endow us with clarity and wisdom. This is new territory for many of us, but we can do all things through Christ that strengthens us. Amen.

There Is a Word

Proverbs 31:16 (NKJV)

> "She considers a field and buys it; From her profits she plants a vineyard."

Chapter 6

Insurance and Retirement—How Much is Enough?

I was recently speaking with an insurance agent, and she said, "Peace of mind is knowing you will not outlive your retirement savings, no matter how the financial markets perform and no matter how long you live." If you want to have this peace of mind, don't leave anything to chance when it comes to retirement income, even within the confines of the church.

As you begin to grow and build your ministry, make sure you have a plan to grow and build your retirement. Too often the vision for the church overrides the vision we should have for our families. No church should exclude from its agenda a retirement package for the pastor and first lady, but neither should you exclude it from yours. Ladies, take a moment and think about what your life would look like if your husband did not make it home today. Really. Stop, think, and see it . . . Are you one of the few who have everything planned so well that all you will miss is your husband's warm body by your side? You will get to stay in the home you love; if you have small children, they can go to the same school and you won't have to worry if you will be able to pay your utilities and bills from month to month.

Or are you one of the many who don't have it all together? You have little life insurance and maybe no retirement. You will not only miss your husband's presence, but you may even have to sell your home, your children may have to change schools, and you will fret from month to month about how you will make ends meet.

So how much is enough? When selecting a plan of security, keep in mind the amount of income you will need to maintain your present lifestyle after he's gone may be as much as 90 percent of your current income. This allotment certainly won't be coming from the church, no matter how many years of service you have given. If you do not have time to save 90 percent of your current income to live on for ten to twenty years after the passing of your husband, adequate life insurance coverage is your only option. Your insurance agent or financial advisor can more explicitly direct you to resources that best suit your needs. Taking a portion of your insurance benefit and placing it in a lifetime income product is a great option to help you guarantee a paycheck for life (Lankford 2010). No matter how you decide to reach your goals, just know that other means of support must, must, *must* be obtained. I am not stuttering. I am simply repeating myself so that you will get into your spirit the urgency of doing what must be done.

So how do you determine how much insurance is enough? You should consider the following:

1) How long do you want to live in the lifestyle you have become accustom to living?
2) Can you pay off your mortgage?
3) Can you pay off any debt?
4) Is there enough money for monthly maintenance?

I am in no way a financial advisor, but I am living life without my husband, and I recommend that there is a minimum of $1 million dollars of insurance coverage on your husband. Never, never consider less than $500,000. If there is only a $100,000 or $200,000 policy and all other means of support stops, you, my sister, will be broke in less than two years. Ask yourself, what will you do then? What will you do if you are unable to re-enter the workforce due to illness or lack of skills or if you are too mature in age? Or maybe you just don't want to go back to work. Ladies, time has certainly brought about change. Be wise with your spending, and do not make any major financial decisions for at least six months. This gives you time to sort things out and make more rational decisions. Take a moment and picture your life without him.

Many of you may have put your dreams on hold so that you could raise your children and help your husband to fulfill his vision. After twenty-plus years, you may have decided to give up your lucrative career so that you could co-labor with your husband in his call for kingdom building. There is absolutely nothing wrong with that if you have prepared for the winter months without him. God always remembers your faithfulness and your work, but others quickly forget about your dedication and sacrifice. They have no empathy for you, regardless of the years you have labored and the service you have given. Enjoy what you and your husband have established together. However, cover yourself so that you will always have enough meal in your barrel. Now, get ready, get set, thrive! Be blessed really well all the days of your life.

Prayer

Oh heavenly Father, thank you for the work you have given these your servants. Teach us, dear Lord, that we may gain a heart of wisdom. Let your wonders give light to our paths that we may walk therein. Our ears are attentive to your directions and our hearts to your will. As we attend to our personal affairs, we acknowledge that you are omniscient and there is nothing hidden from you. Now, Lord, give us the discernment and comprehension to conduct business as we ought so that there will always be enough meal in our barrels.

There Is a Word

Psalm 90:12 (NLT)

> "Teach us to realize the brevity of life, so that we may grow in wisdom."

Chapter 7

Legalize and Notarize

(Promises, Promises)

If by happenstance your husband should die before you, scratch whatever promises were made to take care of you now and forget about those unscripted verbal contracts. They will not hold up in court. Oftentimes people mean well—and I do believe that—but those emotional pledges are seldom, if ever, honored.

The stakes are too high for you and your family to rely upon those undocumented commitments. This is what I call *risky business*. You have worked much too long and too hard to jeopardize your future welfare. Protect yourself and reap the profits of your labor in which you have given of your life. Every man, especially the pastor, should have a legalized truth or documented stipulation stating what will take place regarding his family's welfare at the time of his death. No handshake, secret discussion, or promise is sufficient enough to substantiate your personal financial security. If there is no record, you have no legal ground or recourse on which to stand. No appellant court in that land will uphold a verbal agreement; you must have proper documentation. You need proven evidence on a legalized form to speak for you loud and clear when you don't know what to say yourself. Take time to seek counsel from a *real* attorney. This is not the time to call a friend practicing his street skills. Remember, this could alter your source of income forever, causing you to lose out on what is rightfully yours.

Take action now, and make sure to legalize and notarize what you need to sustain and protect yourself. Notarization ensures the authentication of the signatures on the document and involves an impartial third party. An example of a legal notarized document that would protect you is the ministry's agreement to continue compensation for one year or more upon the death of the pastor. You don't want any more heartache than you already have to bear after losing your loved one. Knowledge is power. The Bible says in Proverbs 22:29, "Seest thou a man diligent in his business" (KJV)?

The problem with church business is there is always transition. People come and go all the time for one reason or another. In the thirty-two years my husband served as pastor, God sent members that stayed until the very end. They helped to set up departments and cabinets; they gave their all and supported the ministry financially. We could always rely on them. These are the folks that gave the church stability.

There were others who came and went all the time for one reason or another. Some of them moved away, some died, and some were only with the ministry for a certain length of time.

Oftentimes the people who signed business papers or kept the books are no longer there when you need, and if you were not a part of the business decisions of the church, you are left in the dark. If that happens, you will have built a ministry and then realize that you know nothing of its business ventures. You have never seen documentation; you have never seen the deeds. Even if discussions are held about the future of the pastor's family, the question would be are those conversations documented? Was a plan put in place, and what do *you* know about the plan?

So often as women we are just having church, working up departments, working up programs, and wearing the first lady hats. I did whatever I had to do, including scrubbing floors, climbing ladders, putting up borders, selling dinners from the trunk of my car to every beauty shop, barber shop, and other businesses in town every weekend, and working two jobs to help with finances as needed.

You are that unsung hero who has endured more than most women will ever endure. The idea that you should leave all the business to your spouse is over. There are too many widows suffering because of this eccentric notion, only to find out at the deaths of their husbands that they are left with nothing but heartache and no future means of support. If I have frightened you, then good! I hope you will now go to your husband and ask again this life-saving question: What happens to me after you are gone?

There is a story about a pastor and his wife who built a successful ministry. They put more than thirty years into this ministry and invested all of their savings into it. After he died, she was offered $400 a month to live on. This stressful situation was totally overwhelming for her. Can you imagine working most of your life, dedicated to kingdom building, and then living below poverty level?

The poignant, antiquated excuse often given when such matters are overlooked is that the widow's husband should have taken care of her. That may be true; some pastors just simply cannot afford large enough life insurance policies to sustain their love ones. Then there are those who just didn't take care of business even though they had plenty of time, and death caught them unprepared, leaving their families utterly distraught. I plead with you to avoid these calamities by making the choice to be a part of your family business and your ministry business. You are not being nosey. You are not in the way. You are wise enough to secure that for which you have labored. Legalize and notarize so that you can reap the rewards of your labor even after he is gone!

As a girl, I knew a prominent first lady who I admired greatly. She and her husband built one of the most successful churches in the area at that time. They had a gorgeous brick home and always kept a beautiful shiny Cadillac, and she was always dressed in the finest clothes and hats. She was a class act, and they both were wonderful people of God. When her husband died, another pastor took over the ministry and forgot all about the widow and her contribution to the building of the ministry he inherited. She eventually moved out of her house into a small apartment, her car was taken, and she never again lived the life to which she had grown accustomed. When she died, the county buried her in a pauper's grave without a headstone. I was only a teenager then, but I can still feel her pain, her loneliness, and her despair. After years of service to building a ministry, bringing souls to Christ, and encouraging and helping others, she lay in an unmarked grave and was put away as if no one remembered her life contributions to that ministry. My heart aches for her, and my spirit is troubled over her devastating last years of life.

I don't know who you are by name, dear sister, but just at the thought of your burdens and the shedding of your tears, you have entered the very essence of my being. I hear you day and night as your wounded soul cry out to God for release from its unrelenting oppression. I write these pages with a pen of hope and a way for you to escape from such unnecessary and unethical miscarriage of justice.

Take the time to officially take care of yourself or else you could find yourself accepting the crumbs from the table you bought and paid for. Make sure your deeds and legal documents can hold up in any appellant court in the land. Keep a copy of everything that you and your husband sign and any other important documents. Know without a shadow of doubt what you are entitled to, and always seek professional counsel.

Prayer

Lord, we thank you for your loving kindness. Keep our minds and our hearts focused on you. Teach us how to conduct our business with wisdom, understanding, and professionalism. Lord, we are grateful for your insight to legalize and notarize as a way to protect the work you have placed in our hands. Because of this endeavor, may there be more gladness than sorrow. Amen.

There Is a Word

Proverbs 3:6 (KJV)

"In all thy ways acknowledge him, and he shall direct thy paths."

Chapter 8
Is There Life After First Lady?

The answer to that most significant and crucial question is a resounding, resolute, decisive *yes*. There is life after first lady! I chose to put the word *decisive* before *yes* because you have to make the decision to live and not just exist as if there is no reason to go on.

The devil is a liar and a deceiver too. You're going to make it with the help of God, and you're going to be all right. It won't be easy, and the hurt is seemingly too overpowering to bear. Know that God will never leave you with nothing. You may feel like you lost it all, so broken on the inside that you can't even get up the next day. But get up anyway. "Do not sorrow, for the joy of the Lord is your strength" (Neh. 8:10b NKJV). By God's grace, you're on the brink of a new beginning. Celebrate where you're going before you get there, and be assured of God's eternal protection. When your heart is overwhelmed and your courage is failing, the

Lord will lead you to a rock of refuge (Ps. 61:2). I know you are hurting, but stand strong, not with your head down but with your head held up!

I will admit that it won't be easy. This is where faith and commitment to God comes into place. "Trust in Him at all times" (Ps. 62:8 KJV). Pour out your heart before Him; God is true to His word, and He sees where you are right now.

Sometimes we women have to pat ourselves on the back and tell ourselves that we can make it. I had to make a destiny decision that I would survive in spite of the drastic change in my life.

Commit yourself to keep moving and not to give in to the dictates of the mind or whines of the flesh. Make a steadfast, unshakable, determined decision not only to survive but to live the abundant life that God has promised each of His children. "The thief does not come except to steal, to kill and to destroy. But I have come that they may have life, and that they may have it more abundantly" (John 10:10 NKJV).

Whatever the age or stage, sister, know that you are more valuable than ever before. You're wiser, stronger, creative, needed, and the Lord will make room for you. He will open doors for you that no enemy can shut. It does not matter what others think of you or what they are saying; God never changes His mind about you. "The eyes of the Lord are on the righteous and His ears are open to their prayers" (1 Pet. 3:12 NKJV). And He will attend to all of your needs.

Search within yourself, find that gift again, and allow God to stir it up with His touch of genius and power.

Four months after my husband's death, I sat there immobilized, observing the installation service of the newly appointed leader. I wondered, *Where do I go from here? How do I walk alone after forty-two years of marriage and thirty-two years in this ministry? Is there a place for former first ladies to go for some type of direction, counseling, or mentoring?* There was none that I could find. I never thought I would be in this place so soon in life after we had worked so hard, but there I was just like hundreds and thousands of others before me. I was listening for God to tell me what to do, and He said it was time to launch Vera Lewis Ministries, "There is a Word," and write this book to enlighten women. Now that I have followed his instructions, I pray that lives will be changed and improved everywhere for the better. Be encouraged, and know that a better-than-right-now is coming!

Life is too short to squander your remaining existence in the valley of despair. There are mountaintop experiences waiting for you. Explore the richer place within yourself that has not been tapped into before.

Create your own identity, and establish your own God-given gifts. I encourage all women to use their first names as well as their last names when introducing themselves. The majority of pastors' wives are called first lady, or they may be called first lady with attachment to their last name only. This is not intended to show lack of respect to your spouse, but it helps to keep who you are alive. Have stationary with your full name on it; have a bank account and at least one credit card in your name. Your gifts and talents do not have to be put on hold just because your husband has been called to the ministry. Be the good first lady; be the good wife; be the good mother; and don't forget to be good to yourself.

Let go, and move on. Put your memories in their proper places, and then you must live. It will not be easy, but with the help of God, you can do it.

Prayer

Lord, I pray that all women who are now starting their lives over would trust you to lead and guide them. Give wisdom to handle every situation they will encounter. Although their spouses are no longer there to provide refuge and protection, you, my Lord, are their constant source of defense. We believe your word: The angels have charge over us to keep us in all our ways (Ps. 91:11). We now give unto thee, the broken pieces of our hearts, minds, and souls. Let the amen of God confirm these words.

There Is a Word

Isaiah 61:3 (NKJV)

"To console those who mourn in Zion, to give them beauty for ashes, the oil of joy for mourning, the garment of praise for the spirit of heaviness."

Appendix –

A Note to the Boaz in Our Lives

Each year, hundreds of men and pastors die, leaving their wives with no means of support. They have usually invested all their life savings into their ministries, making no provisions for retirement or death. Psalm 89:48 says, "No man can live forever. All will die. No one can escape the power of the grave" (NLT)? The problem is that we do not have a clue where, when, or how the angel of death will choose to visit. It has nothing to do with who you are or what you have. It really does not have anything to do with your faith or the anointing upon your life. There are those God chooses to call home at different stages and ages of life. Not only are we to live our lives each day with eternity in view but also with our mortality acknowledged.

At the onset of birth, the process of death begins. That statement is applicable to one and all. Please remember that when this occurs, no one is there to protect or provide for your wife and family after you have gone home to be with the Lord. That charge and obligation has been given to you. It does not matter who you are or what you have; tomorrow is not promised to any of us (James 4:14). One trip to the doctor, one unforeseen incident, or one phone call could change everything in an instant. Don't be caught unprepared for the uncertainties of life's unpredictable upheavals. What a travesty it would be to spend your life—whatever the duration—serving the people, the church, the community, and even the world and become accustomed to a comfortable life here and leave your family struggling to survive after you are gone. Make the wise decision to do the right thing now, and you won't have to worry about the wrong things that could occur to your loved ones later.

Every pastor should remember your partner who co-labored with you through the years: your wife. Let there be no need for offerings at your home going celebrations or the public humiliation of your family facing financial ruin. Knowing that you are great men of distinction, wisdom and character, you should do what is necessary to make provisions for your linage now! A good man leaves an inheritance to his family (Prov. 13:22).

Out of all the wonderful things you have purchased, the greatest gift and most caring expression of love a man could give to his wife is a legalized plan of security that will safeguard and ensure her financial welfare after he is gone.

Even if everything inclusive with the ministry is taken from her, she will be able to continue living the lifestyle in which she deserves to live and worked for as your partner in the vineyard.

You are the Boaz in her life, and she looks to you as her protector and her provider all the days of her life. One cannot help the loneliness that comes after such great loss of a beloved spouse, but certainly something can be done about the status of her security. If you would only prepare for the appointed time that no one can avoid, lonely and broke would not become her lifestyle.

I urge you not to wait another day, for who can discern the times of what is to come? Be blessed real good, you hear!

Prayer

Lord, I pray that every pastor and every man has taken the responsibility and the initiative to place a plan of provision for their families. That it will not be a negotiation but a priority. So there will be no lack or want in their loved ones' daily needs after they have passed from this earth into thine eternity. Father, I pray that these strong, wise, godly men of integrity whom you have called to serve your kingdom will be blessed in their ministries and lives, above and beyond what they could have ever imagined. Amen.

—*Vera L. Lewis*—

There Is a Word

1 Timothy 5:8 (NKJV)

"But if any does not provide for his own, and especially for those of his own house, he hath denied the faith, and is worse than an infidel."

References

MacArthur, John, trans. 1997. *MacArthur Study Bible*. Nashville: Word Publishing.

Stein, Ben. 2010. "For the Sake of Your Loved Ones, Get Life Insurance." *Newsmax.com*, October 25.

Bukow, Tiffany. 2011. "Women and Money—Address Your Needs." *MsMoney.com*, July 12. www.msmoney.com/mm/financial_health/msm_finhealth/_money.

Kiyosaki, Kim. 2011. "6 Reasons Why Women Need to Become Investors." *Empowering Women* 2, no 1, September 4.

Lankford, Kimberly. 2010. "Lock In Your Retirement Income." *Kiplinger's Personal Finance*, May.

All stories related in this book are true, but names have been changed to protect the privacy of the people mentioned.

About the Author

A dynamic speaker, Evangelist Vera Lewis is a compelling spiritual teacher of God's Word. Founder of Vera Lewis Ministries, her mission is to give hope, encouragement, and inspiration to every soul she encounters to survive against all odds and in spite of what has happened to them.

She was saved at the early age of fourteen years old, and God has continued to anoint and use her. She is the cofounder of the Bethlehem Church of God In Christ, located in Fort Worth, Texas, which was founded by her visionary husband, the late Elder James David Lewis.

Evangelist Lewis is a retired nurse and mother of three children. She has dedicated her life to the care of others, both naturally and spiritually. She is the proud grandmother of five grandsons who have already begun to carry out the Lewis tradition of excellence.

She is founder and president of the BIONIC Women of God, an active women's organization that provides Christmas toys, school supplies, and clothes to needy, underprivileged children; Thanksgiving dinners to families in need; and scholarships to deserving students. The BIONIC Women of God are a strong group of women making a difference in today's society.

Evangelist Lewis holds an honorary doctorate degree from the DFW Bible Institute and Seminary. And she is a longtime supporter of Women for Women International Center.

Evangelist Lewis ministers the Word of God on her weekly broadcast, aired on Charter Cable television, in which many souls are saved and blessed. She believes that you can live a saved and prosperous life here on Earth without compromising the gospel. Her messages are spirit filled, and her compassion is heartwarming. Evangelist Lewis delivers a powerful and purposeful message that will change your life forever.

About the Book

Evangelist Vera Lewis has been diligently working on completing her first book since her husband's transition from life on earth to life in glory. Her book empowers every woman, especially pastors' wives, to strategically plan for financial survival after the loss of their husbands. It touches on the severity and unpredictability of life that should encourage us to be prepared both spiritually and economically at all times for whatever befalls us.

Her book was written to jar women into thinking and preparing for life to eliminate the financial hardship and disappointment that women encounter every day because they are not prepared for the unexpected. Too many first ladies are MIA—missing in action—after their lives are so drastically altered.

This book also touches on a specific note to the "Boaz" in our lives, encouraging them to arrange a defined protection plan for their wives and families after they are gone. The greatest gift of love a man can give to his beloved wife is a blueprint for financial security.